SAD FASHIONS

Other titles by Richard Peabody:

I'm in Love with the Morton Salt Girl
D.C. Magazines: A Literary Retrospective (editor)
Mavericks: Nine Independent Publishers (editor)
Echt & Ersatz

POETRY

SAD FASHIONS

RICHARD PEABODY

GUT PUNCH PRESS
CABIN JOHN, MD

For everyone who botched their first kiss, flunked their driver's test, missed the prom or bungled the score that would have won the game.

Some of these poems have appeared in the following places: *Arts/Focus, Beat Scene, Bogg, Chiron Review, Circus Maximus, City Paper (Baltimore), Dog River Review, Folio, Go, Kalliope, Lips, Lithic Review, Maryland Poetry Review, Nightsun, Northern Pleasure, Pig in a Poke, Redstart, Sepia, Union Street Review* and *the Washington Book Review.*

"Arabia Deserta" also appeared in the chapbook *Diet of Earthworms* (Northern Pressure Press, 1985).

"Fumble" also appeared in *The Cooke Book: A Seasoning of Poets* (SCOP Publications, 1987).

First Edition

Library of Congress
Cataloging in Publication No.: 89-8512

ISBN: 0-945144-01-6

Cover Art:
Jody Mussoff
"Hanging Puppet"
1988, colored pencil (27x21)

Gut Punch Press
PO Box 105
Cabin John, MD 20818

Special thanks to Jody for the art, Paul Grant for the cover type, Sunil Freeman and the Writer's Center for the typesetting, and all the friends who read this manuscript in the early stages.

“So leave the ways that are making you be
What you really don’t want to be
Leave the ways that are making you love
What you really don’t want to love.”

— Nick Drake

Contents

III. Nature Morte

AUTHORITY OF FAILURE

"You may ask me why do I fail
just when I'm needed."

— David Sylvian

The Fourth Stooge

When I was five I wanted to be the fourth stooge.
I wanted to be on television and hit Moe with a pie.
I wanted to say nyuk, nyuk, nyuk
and spin around in circles on the floor.
Anything was better than walking to school.

Tommy Cutler and I used to dream about throwing pies
off the top of the Empire State building.
Once, when I was older, I actually hit a kid with a pie.
He threw me across a table. So I gave up
television and became a poet instead.

Now my every word is a soft projectile.

Aging Guitar Player

Looks like he grew up with Elvis.
Riding on the subway with a guitar
case in the aisle. A pot-belly.
Imagine your father as
a professional musician.

Only black men age gracefully.
Chuck Berry playing one-handed
through "Maybellene"
for the zillionth time.

Who knows?
The bald-headed guy
with the shaving kit in one hand,
maybe he's a great guitarist.

The One-Armed Man in Paris

He lives somewhere beneath his skin.
An old buck. Unstable as beer.
Everyone thinks he lost the arm in a fight.
Happened years ago. A debt he couldn't cover.

Now his empty sleeve dangles.
A compass. Memento of lost years.
It's difficult getting a cockeyed
body upstairs. Always drunk.

He remembers knives, and every stranger's eye.
Whets curiosity with a glove tacked where
a fist should be. Shies from the company
of cripples. Balance lies in imbalance.

Why is Other People's Happiness So Hard to Take?

Ball bearings
no longer carry us
without a fuss.

Every touch
the last.

We seek comfort
in new locations.

The sandy outcroppings
of a photo.

Chic formulas won't help.
Too late for that.

Smoke in the bathroom.

Hands reaching up
from under the bed.

A large iquana
tip-tapping
down the hallway.

When I wake up
there is ink
all over my arms.

You've left messages
I cannot decipher.

Victims

She's crying and she
wants me to kill them.
They've called her all
sorts of names, these
real men from the auto
shop across the street.
In my Clint Eastwood
daydreams, I handle it.
I have no mercy.
They die in slow motion
right in front of her.

But in truth I'm powerless
to do anything more than
strut glinty-eyed and cuss.
I can see them laughing.
The same assholes who have
always given me shit
for being short, wearing
glasses and reading books.
I understand those who
go on shooting sprees.
You feel so helpless
in the face of Neanderthal
strength that it just
doesn't matter. You won't
be able to live with yourself
if you take one more insult.
They've already murdered
what's good in you. And
revenge fantasies are the
most common, I've heard.

I'd like all the low-life
pricks who ever gave me
shit to die puking their
guts out.

She's crying.
I'm nobody's hero.
Given the right circumstances
just my being male would
threaten her. And I'm sitting
here worrying about
my own sorry self,
consumed by anger
and guilt and fear.

Stubborn

And again
you force things
that could slide easily.

Why fight it?
The square peg will
never fit the round hole.

Still you stand there
holding a determined hammer
in your hand.

Rats

Tommy and I would sneak off
after *Alfred Hitchcock*
to shoot rats at the dump.
We were twelve or thirteen.
Shivering in the cold,
armed with flashlights and .22s.

You could hear the rats
rustling through the tires and cans.
Feral eyes and teeth.
We'd shine the light
and they'd freeze
so we could pop them off.
The sound so awful clear
in the winter air.

We never brought enough bullets.
That's finally why I quit.
When I thought about how many rats
we must have killed at that dump,
and how many more there were.

Self-Portrait 1969

Each morning
the bite
of broken glass

I'm drunk again

dreaming of
saloon brawls

the mirror
behind the bar

a jigsaw puzzle

my fist fractures
the biggest guy
in the room

contact sports
are all I know
about love

Life After College

Those boys must have been
pretty surprised. They were
really motoring. Don't know
how fast, but headlights shot
out across the community pier
and clean into the water
before I heard screeching tires
or the strain of the engine.

Now it was raining pretty hard
but that's no excuse. When
their Chevelle hit the logs
we've got half-buried to block
off this little dead-end street
I guess it flattened both
front tires and skyrocketed
them about halfway down the pier.

When I heard the crash, well,
that's when I got up from the
t.v. Wasn't a pretty sight.
It was morning before they
could fish them out.

Damage Central

In my life I've broken
nearly everything that was
precious to my mother.
One after another, by accident,
recklessness, or sheer dumb luck.
First the easy stuff—china,
glasses, knickknacks—and
then, one by one, tables,
chairs, lamps.
The family car.

I guess she thought she was safe
after I got out of college,
but one day on a visit home
my brother and I got to tossing
the football around the dining
room. I don't know how it
happened. Seemed like the
most natural thing in the world,
but I can see the ball even now,
soaring out of reach into her
remaining silver candlestick,
the only wedding present
I'd missed, smashing it
completely in two.

My brother and I broke Mom's
heart that day. She
couldn't believe her
two grown sons had done
something so stupid.

Until that moment
I think I believed
my mother had an endless
supply of things she cared about
and that I could never come close
to doing anything that would
ever really hurt her.

Spears of Influence

As I enter your apartment
I understand Fe-Fi-Fo-Fum
for the very first time.

I smell him everywhere.

There's all sorts of evidence:
a hip book or two, some
flowers, cassettes, lp's,
you're even sipping a
different exotic drink.

His fingerprints
are almost tangible.

Time to circle the wagons,
give you my best shot.

But you beat me to the punch
with a startling new vocabulary.

I've gone from good guy
to bad guy so fast
my hands begin to tingle
and as I raise them to eye-level
they vanish.

Hard to believe
it would come to this.

Too late
for a hail mary
miracle.

In seconds
you'll go on
as though
I never even existed.

Have You Seen My Hair Shirt?

Flogging the past is fun!

Her smile crooked
from sleeping alone.

She told me she wanted a ring.
But I was no target
and refused to listen.

"All snapshots fade," she said,
with eyes like dice.
"I never worry about scrapbooks," I said.

Word came that she married.
Life was sex and dinner parties.
I realized my mistake.

The humming air-conditioner
replaces every heartbeat.

And Last in the American League

When I was small
baseball was more important
than girls and Washington
still had a team.

My father used to
take me out
to games at Griffith Stadium.

Any kid who could
walk under the turnstile
got in free.

I stayed small.

Washington has lost
two teams since then
but that doesn't
stop my loving them.

Griffith Stadium
was torn down
and kids have to pay
at other ballparks.

Somewhere along the line
I discovered girls
and grew up.

Now when I watch
a group of kids
swat a ball around

I imagine Bob Allison
getting a piece of one,

and have to fight
this hot-dog craving
for nostalgia—

my city's stolen heart.

A Good Enemy

All you need is one good enemy.
Someone to depend on.
Evil on a grand enough scale
to be a constant target.
So you can bury yourself
in the bull's-eye and
luxuriate in the darkness.
An equal to hone your edges.

But enemies are rare.
The landscape filled
instead with poseurs and
bad boys. They generally
disappoint. Lack a
killer instinct. Have
no staying power.

When you finally discover
a good enemy in your sights
you are surprised to find
them more attractive than
you had hoped.

Perfidy in Amber

Repetition destroys
most relationships.
The same round of stories,
faces and erogenous zones.

Circuits burn out.

It could take two days,
a week, a year. Ten years.
But one day it's chalk
on a blackboard.

Whipped cream won't help.

Disc jockeys playing
songs to death.

I often find myself
humming records I can't stand.

Fumble

In dreams
footballs
one-hop
back to you.
Stickum fingers
hang tight.
Willpower works.

But in games
where control
matters
the pigskin
changes shape
as though possessed,
and rolls
farther away
in slow motion
while the field
telescopes
and bodies
fall.

Another Stupid Haircut

You wish just this once
the mirror would lie.
What was the barber
thinking about?
You felt ridiculous enough
carrying a Peter Gabriel
album into the shop—
visual aids never help.
You clip away with
nail scissors
and soon it looks even worse.
Conservative, square,
totally hopeless,
as though the ones
who cut hair were
really Martians with
only a rudimentary
idea of what humans
are supposed to look like.
Hair like topographic maps,
tv antenna, inverted
umbrellas, poodle dogs . . .
or else the great hair
disaster of Krakatoa—
poking out in
so many directions
that only the
end of the world
will make you feel
at all fashionable.

MYSTERY HIPS

"Oh to die of kisses
ecstasies and charms."

— Scott Walker

Arabia Deserta

Wait for me.

Roll me into your
sleeping bag and
smuggle me past
metal detectors
and customs agents.

When you drink
I want to pour
from the bottle.

When you tug the reins
I want to be
at the other end.

Attached.

As much a part
of you as breath.

Audrey in the Rain

She's not as splashy
as the women I'm
usually obsessed with.
The girl next door
with class. Black gloves.
Eyes in sync with
the orchestration.
A name that implies fashion.

When the sad rains come
she stands breathlessly
perfect, despite
the runny mascara
and tears.
I could freeze-frame
this second
and capture her forever
with a sloppy kiss.

But when I offer
my sorry coat
the patented laughter begins
and those small bones,
those delightful bones,
rattle my heart
until I know
I'm blessed.

Reflex Action

She's shining my shoes again
and I don't know why.
They're still new, black,
barely worn. Couldn't be that dirty.
She likes to do this
to put me off guard (I think).
Her big control number.
She's my little geisha
for a few minutes, hours, years.
I'm supposed to think
yeah, this is "all right,"
"nothing could be better."
But end up asking
why things change
who decides
and what really matters.
She's into the motion now
whipping that cloth back and forth
like a good actress who's seen
too many silent movies
of shoeshine boys
and always wanted to wear a slouch hat
and work in a barber shop.
When she's finished
she'll run to some other man
and leave me here
with shiny shoes,
mementoes
of another life
as archaic
as the love letters
I still write.

The Siamese Twins Are Separated

Once the bond is severed, the utensils
covered with a thin layer of red
there is nothing but stone silence.
For years people have wanted
to go at them with an ax.
"Here, let us fix that little problem for you."
The twins weathered all storms. "We're fine
the way we are," they would say. "We get along."
But the world will have its way sooner or later.
"It's not natural or healthy for two people to be *that* close."

One becomes a martyr. Star of stage and screen.
"You're better off," the voices insist. "We always
hated your twin."

The other revises history. Forgets
there ever was another. Moves away.
Has the baby pictures retouched.

About Blondes

Repeat a pattern
enough times
and image
becomes ritual.

Now you're
getting somewhere.

Hollywood
sells an image:
blondes have
more fun.

You settle in.
Habit becomes
a lukewarm bath.

What's wrong
with the map?
There must be
a destination.

You repeat
the pattern
the ritual

because the image
has undeniable
magnetism

taps into
something glittery
a charm bracelet
fountain of youth

the image
as reward.

Repeat a pattern
enough times
and you're bound
to learn
something.

A Tourniquet for the Heart

after the lust
and trembling

I cut myself

playing scissors
with your smile

Ankle Bracelet

I love
the tiny pearls
of sweat

sizzling
off that golden loop

but I get
to thinking
of cattle brands

and realize
somebody
considers you

property
and doesn't want
you to stray

I'm confident
you're much more

I don't need to
lasso you with gifts
or imagery

Louise Brooks

Her famous
black helmet
triggers autonomy.

A glandular avalanche.

You can relax.
Comb her eyes
for hidden metals.

The war is over.

Telephones ring in all
the holy cities of America.

Torn curtains
hung out to dry
on a windy day.

What Works Best in the Realm of the Heart?

The heart
is a grand liar

capricious shots
crossovers

a prisoner
of familiarity

pain

a black gloved
learning experience

form and function

failure of nerve
failure of imagination

yardsticks
of inability

a fool
in the classic sense

so advertise
negotiate

white flags
and red

indulge
the passive voice

expand
location

drain every cup
playback every melody

Mystery Hips

She looks better
in my Mexican towel
than any woman
has a right to look.

"Sashay" is the word
that comes to mind.
For sashay
she does
into my heart
steaming
fresh from a shower
those orange
and black colors
riding
her hips.

My hands
cool messengers
sliding
down.
I love
that towel
so much
those colors
those hips.

Barbed Wire

so much
held in

so much
kept out

we fold into the
fence many
still mornings

a long drive
with no destination

meandering

striking out

lulling ourselves
into a false
sense of security

nothing is safe
nobody trustworthy

we will be shocked
at how alone we remain
in ten years time

Lady Rayne
Crying Through Heaven

A true mystic's
unappeased hunger
for the infinite

no more wires
whim-whams
aquavit or absinthe

crying through heaven
hidden behind
a libertine's mask

in a moment
the air will fill
with rust

tragic remains

strange gifts
and crazy instruments

conversations with
the word lizard

output consciousness
obscure sources

cigarettes and bandages
coffee and sandwiches

the possible
the probable

tattoos

the ground meat
of souls

can you walk
on your knees?

This Year's Girl

Owns more candles
than she could ever burn.

Amnesia

He thinks about her constantly.
What is she wearing?
Will she sunbathe by the pool?
How late in the day
before she wakes?

He thinks she'll miss
him some. He wonders
what you have to do
in order to stick in
somebody's head?
How to stay there?
Carve a niche for yourself.
Camp out.

He imagines her at
work—a factotum—
and wishes things were different.
He doesn't want to just
blend in with the scenery.
But what else is there really?

A single strand,
pale as frog's eggs,
survives intact
between them.
A shiver could
sever history—
the breath of a third party.
Time has sheltered
this remaining umbilical,
a web so subtle
that neither partner
is really aware

of intimacy,
nor capable of understanding
why it remains.

In sunlight after rain
the thread gleams
and everyone can
see it.
The pair ignore
what connects them
for safety, sanity,
but remain
connected nevertheless.

Prisoners then
they coexist
blind, committed,
innocent.

NATURE MORTE

"I harbour all the same worries as most
the temptations to leave or give up the ghost."

— David Sylvian

The Casket Driver

Horror movies often romanticize
the buggy and myopic horses but
driving caskets has never been
a fashionable job. People are
too superstitious. So a large salary
and benefits has always been necessary.
These days we're ashamed to add
the labels, so hungry men drive
unmarked trucks. The destination
still the same. Why not advertise?
There are many types of death.

The Albatross God

Beating their ridiculous wings
gooney birds lift into the sky
as soon as engines are heard.
They anticipate the arrival
and then they're off—as awkward
and clumsy as kids on Christmas bikes.

Do they consider heaven
as the aircraft sucks them in?
Union with the marvelous?
Or is it all simply bad luck,
an accident waiting to happen,
the landing strip and the birds
victims of propinquity.

No matter—for those who remain
on the ground stare in awe—
as the Albatross god, wounded
engines clogged with feathers
and debris, slides beneath
the implacable water.

The Plague of Dead Fathers

We have reentered the plague years.

Smoke bobs lazily from pyres
where parents burn textbooks
and curse the name of Salinger.

The charnel house is full
but children still seek horror.

Besides, it won't be the kids
next time the dread piper skates
into town, firstborn or otherwise.

And you may rest assured,
it won't be the women either.

No, fathers are trying to sleep tonight
and nothing they cling to will save them.

The Crawfish Man

Lake Ponchartrain is just folding
the sunset in two when you spot him.
A tree stump of a man, so old and gnarled
he could be Creole or Octaroon.

His hair is like a mangrove
and his clothes like sacks
he shuffles and rasps:

"I'm the crawfish man.
Got me some Popeye's fried chicken,
some Mile-Hi pie, a pretty
little filly and a bottle of wine.
Gonna sit out on the pier tonight
and have a good time."

The jazzy chorus trails behind
as he soaks up the shadows
in Jackson Square.

"I'm the crawfish man.
I sucks the heads off crawfish.
I sucks their heads and eats their tails
just like I does my woman.
That's why they call me the crawfish man."

For several minutes, sorcery
exists in your closed universe.
And then it's dark and he's gone.

For Zelda (Forty Years Gone)

We all miss you Zelda.
What were you thinking
as flames consumed the building:

How to make a palette of fire?
How to dance toe-to-toe with death?

He'd been courting you
for some time by then.

I liked you better
as the sunny Confederate belle
before you turned into Ophelia.

So come on back,
tender heart.

Come back
and shake up
our safe little lives.

Edge your way
behind the wheel.

Take us drinking all night,
dancing (though we can
barely walk) and wading
through fountains.

When the sun comes up
we'll share mimosas
on the roof of a hotel
and laugh at stupid jokes.

Zelda, honey,
we all miss you.

Memories just
aren't good enough.

Variations

Apples
on a tree
in a churchyard.

A sugar maple
igniting
October.

Crystal goblets
brimming
with Bordeaux.

A cut
on the lip
of a tiny child.

Signs

He looks like my brother in this dream. Offers me a beer, which I drink. I don't remember very much after that. As though the dream beer was really working that alcoholic magic. But something about my brother begins changing, and I wake up.

Some other time it will be a woman. A close friend. Maybe a girl I took out only once. We'll meet in a shopping mall someplace. All the details correct. The scenery always familiar, and her face will be too, and we'll talk, or go to bed, and I'll get just a flash of something dark, something wrong.

Another night it's my best friend, my most recent obsession, or unrequited love. The incidents always begin with the familiar, and innocently enough so you don't question things until they reach a *certain point*. And then there'll be a misstep. A wrong memory. Like a German soldier not knowing who won the World Series in 1939, or else a friend left-handed now instead of right. I'll get the glimmer of something foul around the edges, so that events run contrary to some unwritten genetic law of my own. And I'll stop.

I worry about what will happen if I don't stop. If I get fooled and fall for it. Or even worse, bored and race on into the darkness. My curiosity's strong but thus far something else is stronger.

The occasional lucky coincidence reinforces any doubts I might have had. The last ticket is purchased right in front of me, or my car gets a flat, and of course I'm upset at the moment but later learn about the tumbling ceiling, or multiple car crash. That kind of thing. It makes me scared to go to sleep sometimes. I sit and read and worry. Not consciously, but kind of on the periphery. Like catching an odd movement in the corner of your eye. Some strange angle that seems out of sync with real life. A cockroach, a busted doll.

The Cruelty Factor

She calls me sister
because I'm gentle
when she's used to violence.

She's jealous of my curly hair,
my narrow hips.
Afraid of my secrets.

This makes me want
to hurt her too.

The Ice-Cream Fiend

She loves ice cream more than anything else.
Follows ice-cream trucks when she spots them
on the road, dreams of Good Humor men who
tie her up, suspend her from the ceiling,
and tickle her with multi-flavored cones.
Without a spoonful she's insecure. Buys her
lovers ice-cream scented shirts, ties,
and after-shave. Eventually marries a guy
who owns a dairy. Makes him wear a vanilla suit.
And for a present demands an ice-cream cake
as big as the White House. Gets it.
Honeymoons in Hershey Park, Pennsylvania.
Drowns in a pool of chocolate mint.

The Death of Smith-Corona

Somebody has unraveled cartridges
and draped the black tape
on a wooden cross
in the freshly exposed cornfield.
There are machine parts in the furrows.

Writers congregate on the horizon
beside your stalled Porsche.
They have run out of ribbon
for the last time.

"There was no guarantee the cartridges
would last," you shout. "No crime
in better means of communication."

The black hood they carry is for you.
The shotguns are not props. They have more
than typing on their minds right now.

Glasgow Kisses

They say that
language is truth,
that words really matter.
So I want to know—
if I say I hate you
enough times
and write it
in enough places
will you bend
over clutching
your sides and die?
I mean, what are
the limits?
How many times
must I say it?
Ten? Twenty?
A hundred?
Does it matter where?
And what then?
If I whisper that
I hate you
rest assured that
I'm telling the truth.
Language is your guide.
And I just can't stop
thinking about you.
If you ever encounter
any trouble in
your life—
I want you to
know it comes
with a kiss.

Lorenzo

The path is muddy and the rain
so hard that you forget about
visiting—perhaps tonight
she'll come to you.

Moorgreen waits, watches,
promises to swallow both you
and your characters someday,
if the mine doesn't get them first.
And the mine may be dark but you can hear
Vulcan's hammer faintly ringing.

Better turn back. Back to your writing pad.
She will come tonight, you're sure.
Row houses gleam in clay-washed rain glow.

Lost Messages

My phone machine
swallows your voice
as the tape runs out
on your first few words.
I've never known you
at a loss for words
and the fact that
my phone machine has
sabotaged this—our first
actual contact in over
three years—is more
than I can bear.

I'm holding my breath.
I haven't really heard
your voice in so long—
I wasn't even sure it was you—
rifling through the speech
patterns in my memory bank
until the right combination
popped into place.

I keep rewinding the tape.
Replaying the inscrutable fragment.

Antiquated equipment.
I should probably buy a new machine
but it's too late now.
Of course, I don't have the
faintest idea why you called.

I suppose after a tease
like this—no message
could have been good enough.
No dying cat, or relative,
no broken heart, or job offer,
nothing—not even the promise
of amnesty, or your undying
love for me. It's not fair.
I have no way to reach you.
Don't know where you live.
Another letter lost by the
post office, buried in some
back yard, delivered years
later—you'll never know
that I would have called
you back, craved the contact.

Memory Babe

Jack!
The toaster won't toast
and I'm sitting here goopy
at three in the morning
thinking about you.

You remembered every
conversation you'd ever heard
though sometimes you
couldn't find your way home.

Who would've thought
a jock would write books.

But you said it.
You played time's harmonica
down rainbow splattered
Lowell streets.
You sang the babble babble
of words. Hitched your dreams
to typewriter keys and
fed the world your soul.

King of the Barrel

My uncle
drove a motorcycle
in a barrel

at county fairs
he commanded
every eye.

Defying gravity,
leaving black streaks
on slick wood

like some
grounded astronaut.

It was nothing
he told me.

Sometimes
there were
three bikes.

The one in the middle
ran the opposite
direction.

Crowds
would urge them
to drive faster,

wishing for accidents.

But in that circular world
my uncle was a speed king,

stealing children's hearts,
caressing older sisters.

Rescued By Saxophones

Just when I'm thinking
AM radio has got to be
better than lite rock
I hit a gap between signals.

Static.

Next thing I know,
faintly at first,
as though the transmission
originated on Planet Jazz,
I detect something
and then there's
no mistaking—
it's Ornette Coleman.

And North Platte
doesn't look so impossible
after all.

Seasons of Midgets

People scatter as the Stuka pilot
completes his run. Every connection is filled.
Synapses snap like hot sausage.
A master of interstices, *his*
is the perfect angle of descent.

The Pygmies are playing Avalon Hill
war games. Size has become tactical
once more. Bone elongation is the
latest atrocity.

Farolitos

Nobody will get
any sleep tonight.

It's Christmas
and New Mexico
has become
a giant birthday cake.

Bags of light
materialize
on the flat
crow's nest
of each roof,
each window.

A delicate
geometry.

As I race
the moon
up highway 68
to Taos
I think of
the party scene
in *Le Grand Meaulnes*.

Every desert town
signalling
like some
strange ship.

The snow
tumbling
down.

photo by Carmen Reyes

Richard Peabody is a DC native. He was editor/publisher of *Gargoyle Magazine* for fourteen years. His poems, stories, essays and reviews have appeared in the *Baltimore Sun, City Paper, Columbus Dispatch, Fiction Writer's Market, Washington Post Book World, Washington Review, the Washingtonian* and *WETA Magazine* among others.